BOOKWORMS

Animal Homes

A Gorilla's Nest

Arthur Best

Cavendish Square
New York

Published in 2019 by Cavendish Square Publishing, LLC
243 5th Avenue, Suite 136, New York, NY 10016

First Edition

Library of Congress Cataloging-in-Publication Data

Names: Best, B. J., 1976- author.
Title: A Gorilla's Nest / Arthur Best.
Description: First edition. | New York : Cavendish Square, [2019] |
Series: Animal Homes | Audience: K to grade 2.
Identifiers: LCCN 2017059667 (print) | LCCN 2017060179 (ebook) | ISBN 9781502636676 (ebook) |
ISBN 9781502636669 (library bound) | ISBN 9781502636683 (pbk.) | ISBN 9781502636690 (6 pack)
Subjects: LCSH: Gorilla--Nests--Juvenile literature. | Gorilla--Behavior--Juvenile literature.
Classification: LCC QL737.P94 (ebook) | LCC QL737.P94 B47 2019 (print) | DDC 599.884156--dc23
LC record available at https://lccn.loc.gov/2017059667

Editorial Director: David McNamara
Copy Editor: Rebecca Rohan
Associate Art Director: Amy Greenan
Designer: Megan Metté
Production Coordinator: Karol Szymczuk
Photo Research: J8 Media

The photographs in this book are used by permission and through the courtesy of: Cover Stephen N Haynes/Shutterstock.com; p. 5 Paula French/EyeEm/Getty Images; p. 7 expictura/iStock; p. 9 Gerard Lacz/VWPics/Newscom; p. 11 Reynold Sumayku/Alamy Stock Photo; p. 13 Veronique Durruty/Gamma-Rapho/Getty Images; p. 15 Martin Harvey/Gallo Images/Getty Images; p. 17 erwinf/Shutterstock.com; p. 19 DaveThomasN/iStock; p. 21 Mary Ann McDonald/Visuals Unlimited, Inc./Getty Images.

Printed in the United States of America

Contents

A gorilla is an **ape**.

Gorillas are tall.

They are big.

They are black.

Gorillas look like monkeys.

But they are not.

They do not have tails.

Gorillas make **nests**.

They are like the nests of birds.

But the nests are big!

Gorillas use plants to make a nest.

They use grass.

They use **branches**.

A nest keeps a gorilla safe.

Some nests are on the ground.

Some are in trees!

Gorillas sleep in their nests.

They sleep at night.

Most gorillas sleep **alone**.

But mothers sleep with babies.

Gorillas **wake** in the morning.

They move.

They find food.

Soon it will be night.

Gorillas will make new nests.

They will have new homes!

New Words

alone (uh-LOHN) With no one else.

ape (EYP) An animal that looks like a monkey but has no tail. Gorillas are apes.

branches (BRAN-chez) Long sticks on a tree.

nests (NEHSTS) Beds.

wake (WEYK) Get up.

Index

About the Author

Arthur Best lives in Wisconsin with his wife and son. He has written many other books for children. He sees gorillas at the zoo.

About BOOKWORMS

Bookworms help independent readers gain reading confidence through high-frequency words, simple sentences, and strong picture/text support. Each book explores a concept that helps children relate what they read to the world they live in.